Other books by Benjamin Chan

Grandfather's Old House
High Desert
The Candle Burns at Both Ends
Death Threats for Breakfast
The Birdwatcher
The Flight of the Green Heron
Enter Kyoto

Life is a Camera

Benjamin Chan

Disclaimer

This is not a how-to book, nor is it a self help book.

Dedication

To my Sensei

Maribeth Tik

You may not know it but your words and
questions gave me great guidance.

"Life is like a camera. Just focus on what's important and capture the good times, develop from the negatives and if things don't work out, just take another shot."
— **Unknown**

Introduction

Yesterday, I attended my daughter's commencement program at University of New Mexico. It pulled me back to 1982 when I graduated with a degree in Biology. I started my journey to the top.

What was the top as described by others?

My father pointed to where the rich people lived in Manila. "Look, many of them are doctors."

Then there was the American dream. Have a house, have a car, have a job and have a family.

Twenty years later, in 2002, I reached the top. I was a doctor. I had a house, a car, a job and a family. However, my life was miserable. Was it the top that my father and other people described? What did I miss? I worked hard. I studied hard. I reached the top and it was

empty. I walked out from my marriage. It was a full blown midlife crisis.

A month ago, I reposted the following picture in my Facebook page.

It was a picture I took in my apartment when I first moved to Las Vegas in 2016. I was working on my memoir at that time.

I also added the following text:

The Candle Burns at Both Ends

Until one day I wake up
to find out
I used up all my energy
pursuing
climbing
and reaching
the mountain top
and it is empty

Before long, my sensei posted a question:

Sensei: What did you expect to find at the top?

And it led to the following conversation:

Me: Happiness, fulfillment 😊

Sensei: Do you mean you felt no happiness at all along the way? No sense of accomplishment or pride in the steps that led to the top? No joy in the friends and people you met along the way?

Me: Good question. I think that's where the problem is, focusing on the outcome. Yes, there is an accomplishment. But the daily emotional turmoil made it insignificant ☺

Sensei: You are a great photographer Benjie. Finding happiness daily follows the same principles you use to take great photographs. Here are some:
1) You can see angles that I wouldn't have ever thought would look good or interesting.
2) You can zoom in on something so small and fade out the background.
3) You play with lighting to make something that's not so beautiful, stunning.
See if you can make the analogies to life that I have not said but hopefully implied.

Me: Thank you sensei!

That conversation caught my attention. It was another AHA moment in my life.

How did I miss all those things along the way to the top?

It also stopped me and made me think about the techniques I used for my photography. The most common one that I used when I am stuck in a photo session is FOLLOW THE LIGHT. I found out that if I just follow the light, it will always show me something interesting to shoot.

The next day, my sensei added the following:

"And since you are the cameraman, the one that has the power to decide which photos to take and which ones to discard, you have life in your fingertips. It's your choice. It's your camera. It's your eyes that see what you want to see!"

So how do I apply those strategies to life?

That is the purpose of this book.

Photography Lesson 1

The Right Setting

In a manual setting, it is important to check the aperture and the speed. For aperture, the higher the number, the smaller is the opening, which means that it will allow less light to come in, which means that the picture will be less bright.

The sun was bright when I took the above picture. I also put the camera right under the sun. The initial aperture was set at 4. The opening was too big, thus too much light came in and thus too bright. I had to change it to 14 later.

The other factor is speed. The lower the number, the slower is the opening and closing of the shutter, which allows more light to come in. Again, the initial setting was 100. I changed it to 500.

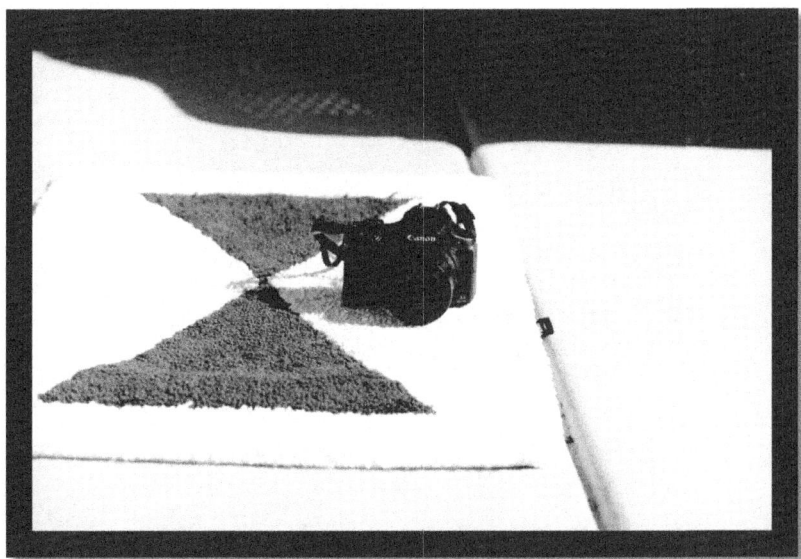

So after changing the aperture to 14 and the speed to 500, the picture was better.

Of course, I can always put setting to auto and the setting will be adjusted but that's not what happened in life. Actually, living our life in auto setting can lead to problems.

"Photography for me is not looking, it's feeling. If you can't feel what you're looking at, then you're never going to get others to feel anything when they look at your pictures."
— **Don McCullin**

Life Strategy 1

Adjust the Setting

In the past years, I had been searching for ways to change the setting of my life. When I hit midlife crisis, I knew that I had to make a change.

Few years ago, I found a coach who used to be a practicing physician. The time with him taught me the following lesson.

"Burnout is not a problem. A problem is like an abscess. You cut it out and it is gone forever. Burnout is a dilemma. It means that you have to constant balance your life."

Constantly balancing our life means that we cannot be constantly on auto mode. We need to change the aperture and the speed.

Visiting the Strip in Las Vegas is a great example of sensory overload. The bright neon lights and the loud music can drown you and let you lose your focus. That is the reason why the place is always packed with people. It is a good place to escape. But as we know, escaping once a year is not the solution. The balancing act needs to happen in a daily basis.

Over the years, I tired many activities to balance my life. I tried yoga, meditation, ikebana, triathlon, golf and photography. During my recent trip to Kyoto, Japan, I learned the tea ceremony. I also bought a set of bowl and matcha for my own tea ceremony at home.

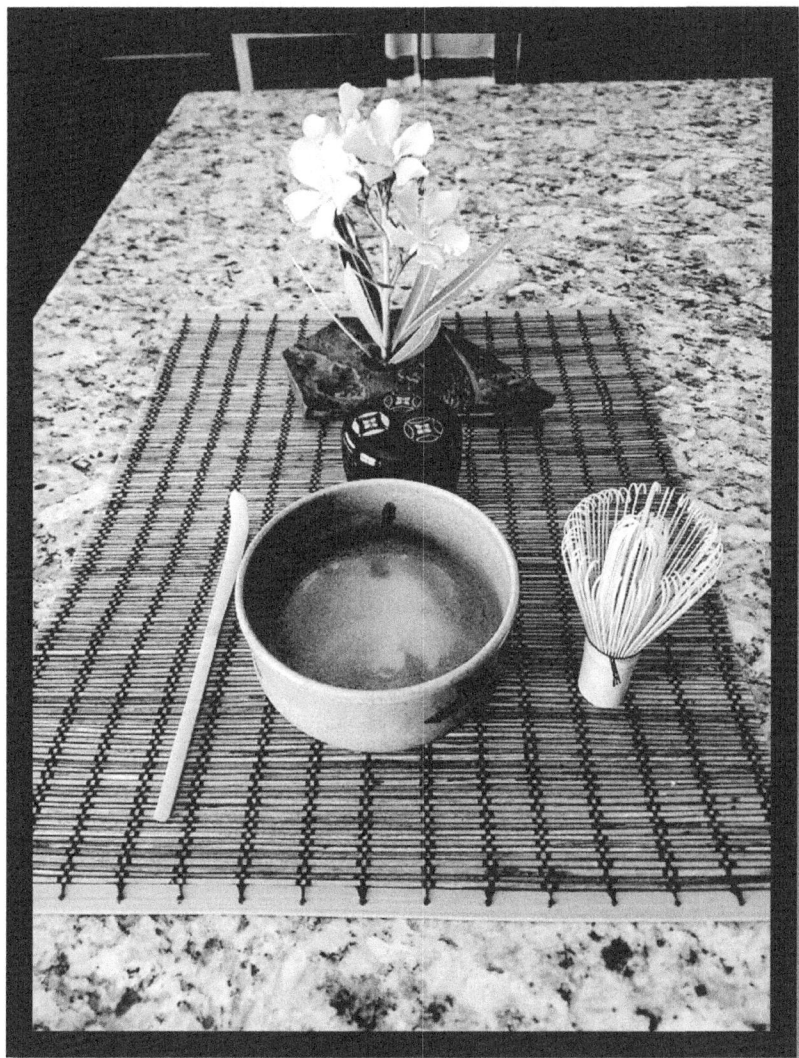

As I said earlier, it has to be a daily act of balancing. Waiting for the yearly vacation or retirement is not going to do it.

It does not have to be long. Some times a few minutes will do.

The key is to have the awareness and the intention to do it.

Photography Lesson 2

Angle

After adjusting the setting of the camera, a simple next step is to try different angles to take a picture of the subject.

Angle 1: from the top

Angle 2: Eye Level

Angle 3: From below

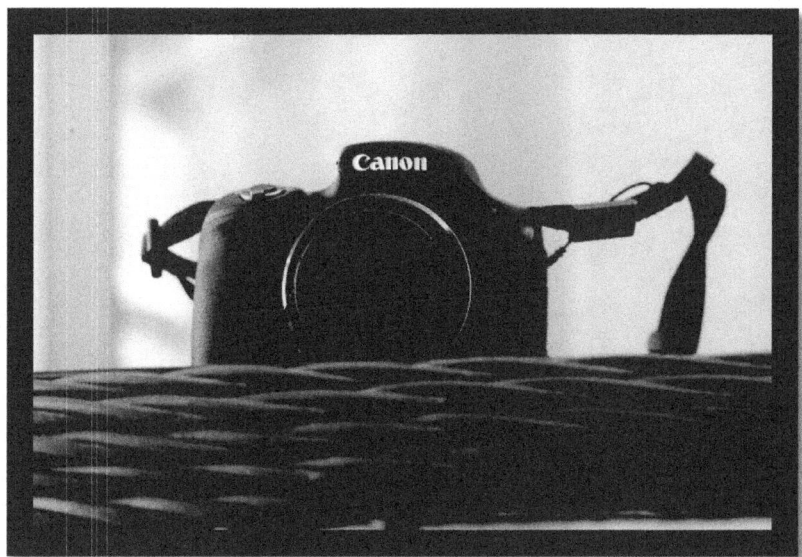

See how different it looks.

You may ask, "So which is better?"

The answer is, "It depends."

What are you looking for? What are you going to use the photograph for?

From an artistic point of view, I will choose angle 3. For me, it just looks better.

"I never have taken a picture I've intended. They're always better or worse."
— **Diane Arbus**

Life Strategy 2

Different Levels

The biggest source of my unhappiness these days is my medical career.

The medical profession has changed a lot since I completed my medical education in 1987.

Most physicians in America these days are so called employed physicians. We belong to a system. We go to work, get our pay check every two weeks and report to our managers.

The insurance company dictated what we can do. They pay what they want to pay. They approve or deny a medication that I prescribe. I have to ask for PTO to go on a vacation. My bonus is determined by my manager. Patient satisfaction survey score is a big determining factor in my bonus.

As I look at this issue today, bearing in mind what I just said about using the angle approach of photography, I can see three levels.

Level one is from above. I see myself going to work four days a week. I did not have to be on call anymore. I see the benefit of being off every Wednesday. I also see the benefit of having a manager who will need to fix any problem that arises form the office. All I needed to do is go to work, see patients, do the paperwork and then go home. When the toilet is broken, call the manager. When the light bulb is broken, call the manager. When the alarm is not working, call the manager.

Level two is at eye level. I see myself sweating over the small stuff. The computer is not working. The insurance company denied the prescription. The referral office asked me to do this and that before willing to process the referral. The patient gave me a bad review. I have to review thirty lab reports. This does not look fun.

Level three is a view from below. I see my son who is getting ready to take his MCAT. It is an examination which will determine if he can get into medical school or not. I also see other medical students in the Philippines who hope to come to America one day. I am way passed that stage. I am actually in the last ten years of my medical career. Everything is relative. I need to remember that.

So what is the result of this exercise? I feel better. I kept forgetting this point of view. Writing about it helps me remember and feel it.

Photography Lesson 3

Zoom In

I love to zoom into the details of my subject. It is one way for me to see the tree and not the forest. I also love to use the soft focus feature of my Picasa photo editing program.

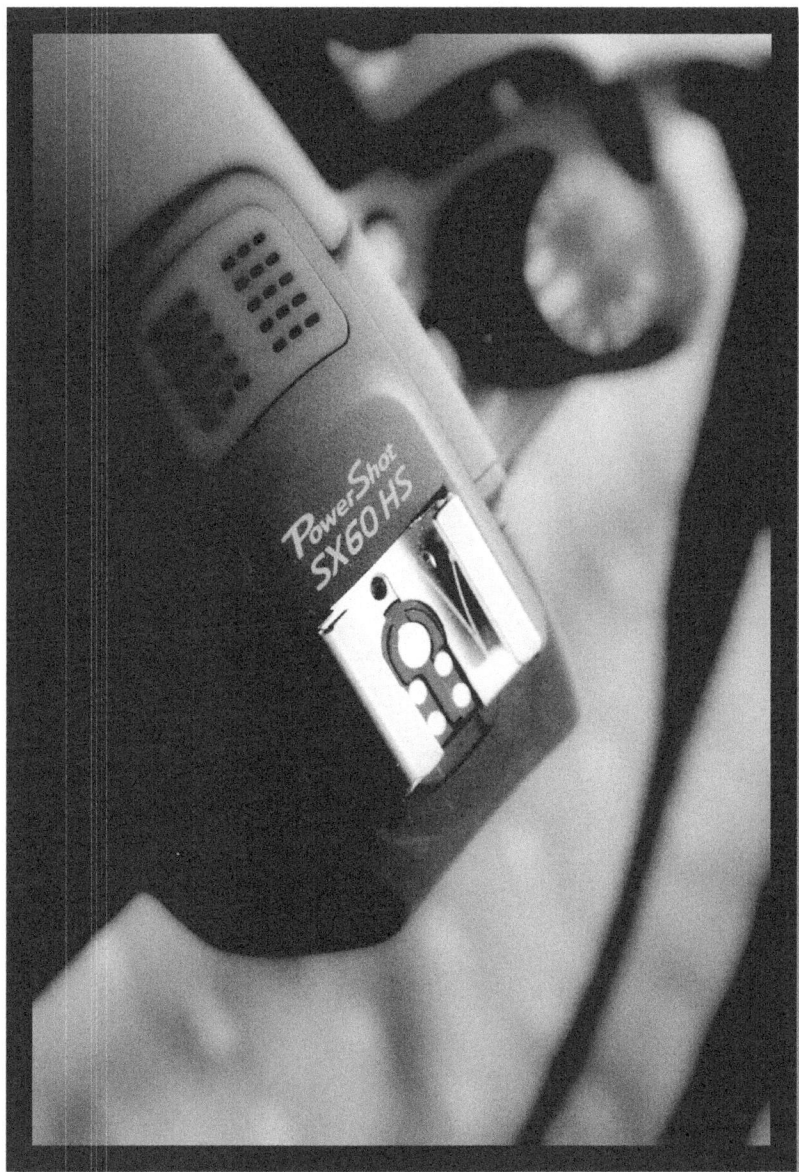

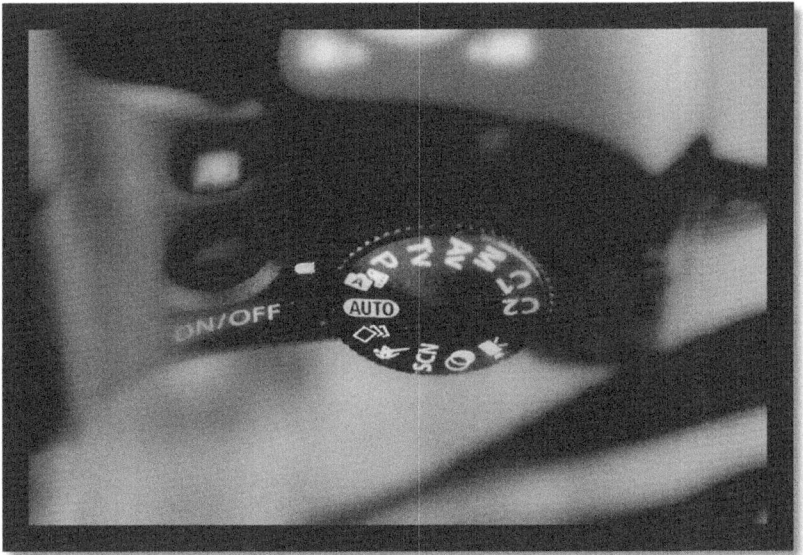

"My life is shaped by the urgent need to wander and observe, and my camera is my passport."
— **Steve McCurry**

Life Strategy 3

Blocking out the Surrounding

When there are too many things in our mind, it is difficult to see what is important. Zooming helps us clear the mind and prioritize.

In my thirty years of medical practice, what stood out was the CPR I did recently.

I was in an examination room visiting with a patient. Suddenly, there was a knock at the door.

"Come in," I said.

Our phlebotomist opened the door and quickly said, "We need you."

I stood up and hesitantly walked towards the door. It could be anything. It could be that she needed an order for me to draw the blood. It could be that we need to add an order. It could be that a patient showed up without an order. Or it could be that the patient was not fasting and insist that blood be drawn.

I followed her to the blood drawing station. When I stepped into the room, I saw on elderly lady in the chair. Her head was tilted behind. Her mouth opened. The face was ash grey. Not a good sign!

I grabbed her hand and using the tip of my nail, pinched the end of her nail. That was a very painful stimulation. Over the years, in a situation like that, the patient will regain their consciousness.

She did not. Another bad sign!

I looked at the phlebotomist. "Call 911!"

I then zoomed into the task in front of me.

"Let's put her on the floor," I told the nurse who was checking her blood pressure.

After we put her on the floor, I wasted no time and started chest compression. The nurse got the ambu-bag and started giving her blows of air.

We worked as a team. After I gave ten compressions, she would give two blows of air.

The medical assistant came in and started monitoring her pulse and oxygen level with an oximeter.

After four cycles, the medical assistant yelled, "She has a pulse!"

Then the nurse said, "She is breathing!"

We paused.

I noticed that the color of her face turned reddish. She was taking her own breath. The oximeter registered a reading. There was a heart rate.

Zooming in saved the life of that patient.

When I talked to the staff after the incident, they mentioned all the other things that happened during the CPR. I did not notice those. All I focused on was my chest compressions.

Photography Lesson 4

Follow the Light

When I look at a subject, the first thing I look for is the source of light. No matter how beautiful a subject is, if the light is behind it, the subject looks dark and will lose all its beauty and details.

Of course we are talking about natural light, without the use of reflector and artificial light.

Let's look at two photographs. The first one has the light behind it and the second has the light into it.

The strategy seems to be simple but often times, we forgot about it.

"Photography is the story I fail to put into words."
— Destin Sparks

Life Strategy 4

The Light

Hindsight is 20/20. Life lessons are 20/20. It is easier to understand life when we look back. However, we live life forward.

The key is to remember what we learned from our past. As someone said, "A mistake is only a mistake if we do not learn from it. Otherwise, it is a lesson."

Looking back, I learned that no matter how "dark" a situation is, there is always a light somewhere.

We just did not see it.

When the "sky fell", when a close family member died, when we lost something, when we lost everything, when we became ill, when our career came to a complete stop, all we see and feel is complete darkness.

But even in the darkest time of all, there is light.

When my girlfriend left for another country during my second year medical school, the "sky fell". I almost dropped out of school.

Looking back, the light came in a form of friendship. People next to me who were willing to help. People next to me who were willing to extend a hand. A friend gave me money to buy a plane ticket. I got the money but eventually did not use it. My close friend David stopped me. David took the time to have a heart to heart talk with me. I stayed and continued my schooling.

If I were to leave medical school, I do not know what I would be doing now in Central America.

Love. Friendship. Hope.

The light is always there. We just have to learn to stop, clear our vision to see it.

"When I photograph, what I'm really doing is seeking answers to things."
— **Wynn Bullock**

.

Photography Lesson 5

Crop

To crop is to use simple and free editing applications like Picasa to cut out part of the photograph.

The above is a photograph I took in Kyoto, Japan. I love the pitched roof of the temple but I got two so called photo bombers in the right lower section.

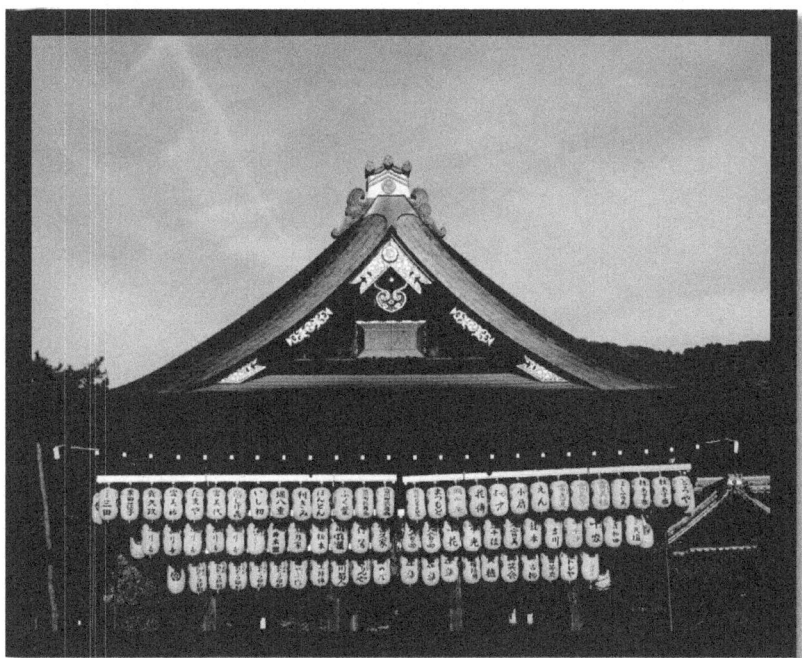

With the use of crop in Picasa, I was able to clean out the photograph. Now the viewer can focus on the beautiful temple and not get distracted by the two tourists.

Agree?

"When words become unclear, I shall focus with photographs. When images become inadequate, I shall be content with silence."
— **Ansel Adams**

Life Strategy 5

Trimming Relationships

How do I apply the concept of "crop" in my life?

I do it by trimming my relationships.

I took a good look at my life and my relationships. I found out that I kept a few relationships because we were blood related and just because even the relationship did not feel right, I did not take the time to clean out.

Last year, I started the process. I released people with negative energies from my life. Life without them is not perfect but at least I cut down some sources of negativity.

Life is short. Life is hard and challenging. I want to save my energies and also attract more positive energies.

"In photography there is a reality so subtle that it becomes more real than reality."
— **Alfred Stieglitz**

Photography Lesson 6

Off Center

In taking a picture, the usual instinct is to put the subject right in the middle. Most photography books suggest an off center approach.

The above photograph was taken in Ryoanji Temple in Kyoto, Japan.

See the big rock right in the middle of the photograph?

With use of crop editing process, I cleaned out the surrounding and move the rock off center.

Better?

"Taking an image, freezing a moment, reveals how rich reality truly is."
— **Anonymous**

Life Strategy 6

Not Taking the Center Stage

Life can be better sometimes when we stay away from limelight.

When I was growing up, getting famous and rich like the Hollywood stars or professional sport players sounded like a great proposition.

However, as I follow my idols through out the years, I found out that they paid dearly for being famous. Tiger Woods, who made millions of dollars playing golf, bought a boat and named it Privacy.

When I was growing up, I won many awards and was known to make many trips to the stage during commencement ceremonies. I always felt uneasy walking down the stage. I could feel that thousands of eyes were staring at me. One time, I had the courage to look up and look at the audience. I found out that they actually busy talking and not watching me.

Staying off the center stage can give us the chance to enjoy the moment. We do not have to worry about our acceptance speech. We can relax, people watch and who knows, find something interesting!

"Once you learn to care, you can record images with your mind or on film. There is no difference between the two."

— **Anonymous**

Photography Lesson 7

Break the Rule

It is true that off center subject can be seen better but sometimes we can break the rule.

Know the rule and break the rule sometimes.

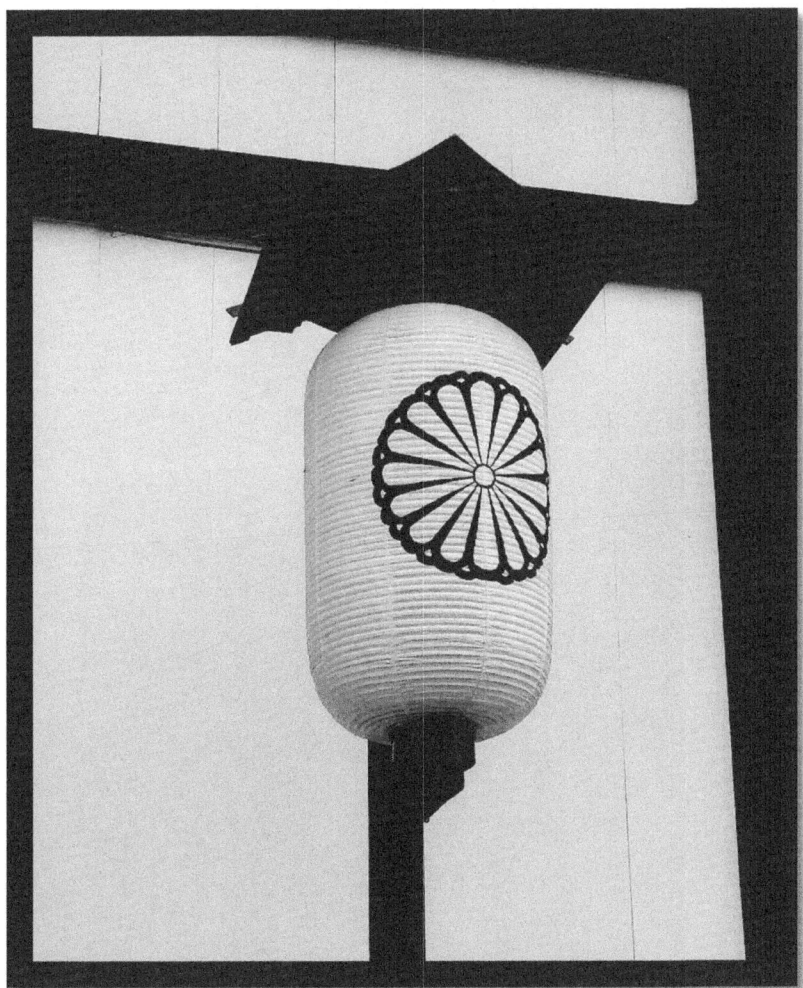

"There is one thing the photograph must contain, the humanity of the moment."
— **Robert Frank**

Life Strategy 7

Side Stepping

Knowing the rule and then break the rule.

This is different from knowing the law of the country and breaking it.

The rule which I grew up with was the old tradition handed down from generations to generations. It was the rule from old China, carried by my grandfather when he crossed the Pacific Ocean and went to the Philippine to seek better life. There was famine and death in southeast China at the time.

The rules were passed to my father, then to me. It was partly an authoritarian view point. One of it was like, "I am the elder or father. You follow what I tell you to do."

In hindsight, it was correct. My father led me to a path of medicine. I survived the training and is now reaping its benefits. Sitting here in my study room, typing at peace and at ease, I thanked my father for his guidance.

However, I did not apply that rule to my son and daughter. I only have one suggestion. Learn a

skill which will support yourself financially, because I may not be around.

I had several talks with my son about his desire to go to medical school. In a way I know that it is a safe profession which would survive any economic meltdown. On the other hand, I just did not want him to go through what I went through.

So far he is determined to continue. I support him a hundred percent.

As for my daughter, she started as an engineering major. She wanted to be an environmental scientist. After stepping into the university world, she changed. She became a math major. She spent her junior year in Germany. She found a way to get a scholarship while studying there.

She is now interested in museum work, which I think is a lovely idea.

Rules or traditions are meant to be carried, executed and passed to the next generation. However, just like photography, you can side step it from time to time.

Photography Lesson 8

Keep the Background Simple

It is important to watch the background of our subject. We want our subject to stand out.

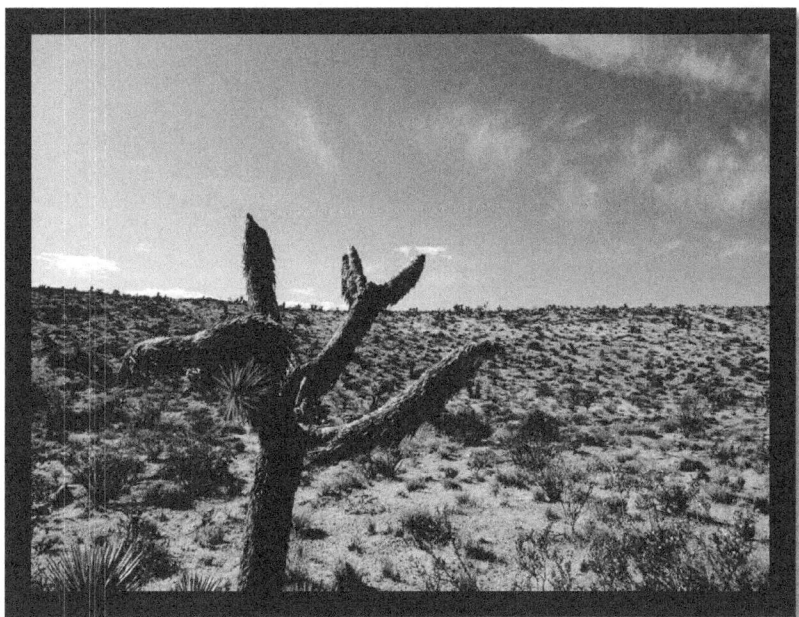

The above photograph has its background covered with the desert ground.

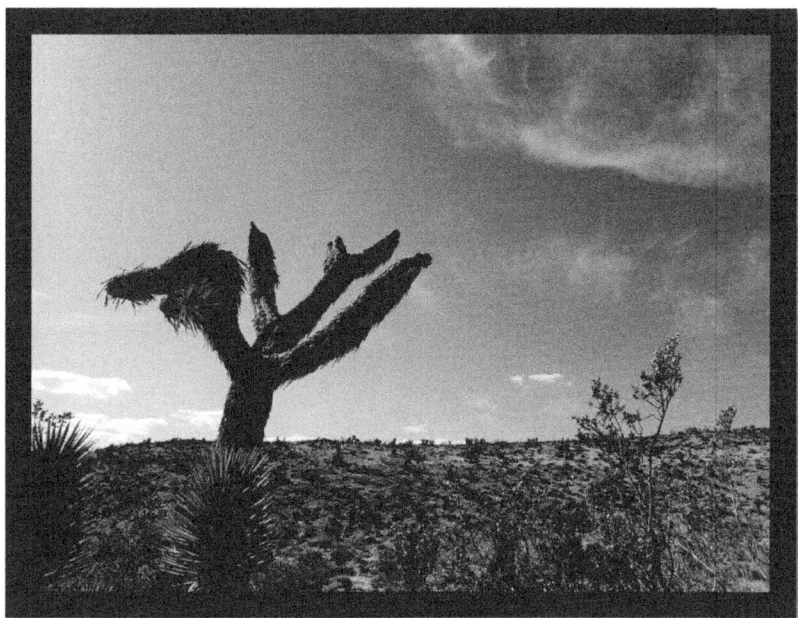

With the second photograph, I took it from a different angle. It used the sky as its background. And it made the desert plant stand out more.

"To me, photography is an art of observation. It's about finding something interesting in an ordinary place... I've found it has little to do with the things you see and everything to do with the way you see them."
— **Elliott Erwitt**

Life Strategy 8

Declutter

There is a need for space for the energy to flow.

That is another thing that my wife and I have in common. We do regular decluttering.

When we moved from New Mexico to Nevada two years ago, I made many trips to Goodwill. One strategy was to downsize from a four-bedroom house to a two-bedroom apartment. It was not easy. It was painful. It was worth it.

More and more people are now talking about energy flow. From China's practice of acupuncture and Feng Shui, to the concept of the Universe made up of atoms and energy.

As a physician, what I see the most in the outpatient setting is anxiety and depression. Many people are stuck emotionally. Their energy flow is also not every good.

Imagine waking up to a house that is clear of clutter. The sunlight comes in. The house is bright. When you open the door, the energy flows freely into the house. It flows through you, charge up your atoms, allowing you to go through your day with ease.

There are different ways to declutter.

1. Get a box, put things inside, seal it and date it. If you did not open it in a year, bring the whole box to the donation center.
2. Think before you buy. I used to buy souvenirs during my travel. Now I do not. The best souvenir is fully experiencing the place. It will stay in your memory.
3. When you buy something new, get rid of something old.
4. Downsize. Move to a smaller house.
5. Spring cleaning. Clean the house inside out. Remove trash.
6. Simplify. Can you borrow instead of buy?

Photography Lesson 9

The Best Camera

Over the years, I searched for the best camera. I had a notion that I needed the best camera I can afford to take good pictures. To some degree, it is true.

Somewhere along the search, someone said, "What is the best camera? It is the camera that you had with you."

It is very true. I have two cameras right now. One is the heavy Nikon DLSR and the other one is the lighter Canon Powershot.

This morning, I decided to take a walk in the desert. I did not want to carry more than what I needed. I left the camera at home.

About half a mile into my walk, I saw something interesting. A deserted car! So with the only camera I had, a smartphone, I took a picture.

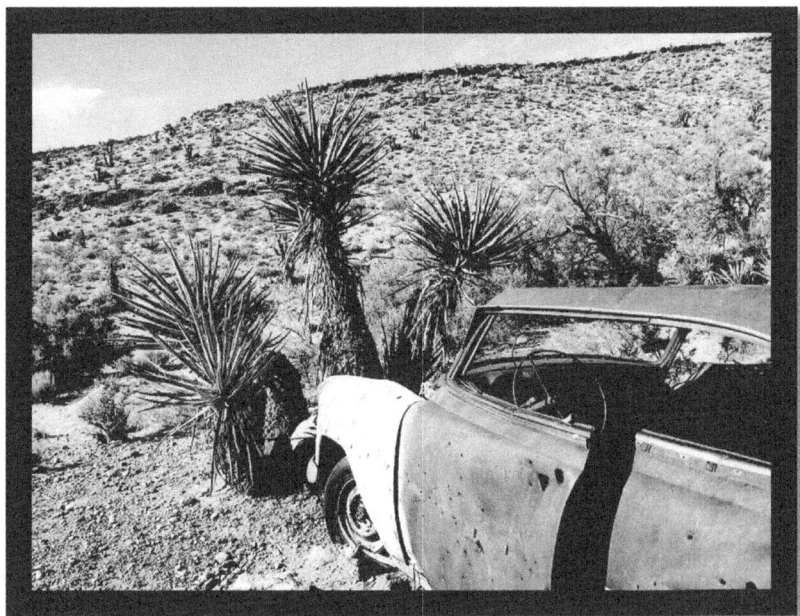

"We are making photographs to understand what our lives mean to us."
— **Ralph Hattersley**

Life Strategy 9

Be Present

As a physician, I have the wonderful experience of seeing humans take his first breath and also his last breath.

The first one was exciting. After a hard passage through the mother's tight canal, he came out and took his breath with a big cry.

The second one was peaceful. He tried his best. I tried my best. It was time to leave this so called life with memories and lessons that were meant to be.

The point is, I need to be present.

What if I quit medical school before we got to the clinical rotations? What if I did not show up that day in my OB rotation? What if I decided to ask my partner to take care of the dying patient? What if I completed my medical education but did not practice medicine?

There are many events in life that are truly breathtaking and will leave a deep impression if we make the effort to be there.

Taking a long hike.
Being a Boy Scout.
Sharing poems with friends.
Attending a book launch.
The first kiss.
The first embrace.
Watching your child graduate from college.
Feeding a deer.
Soak in sea water.
Holding a real katana.
Sitting in silence for ten days.
Swim, bike and run.
Watching the sunrise.
Watching the sunset.
Seeing the underwater in a small submarine.
Seeing four shades of ocean blue and green.
Drinking beer with lemonade.
Sleeping inside a tent.

Photography Lesson 10

Repetition

It is nice to see a single subject stands out. It is also nice to see multiple subjects in repetitive order.

197

"The picture that you took with your camera is the imagination you want to create with reality."
— **Scott Lorenzo**

Life Strategy 10

Routine

I am a golfer. When I play a round of golf, I go through something called the preshot routine.

When I stand on the tee box, I choose a target. It can be a tree at the end of the fairway or maybe the roof of those houses on the side of the fairway.

I make a practice swing. Then holding the driver in front of me, I align the ball and the target using the shaft, then I pick an intermediate target. It can be a leaf, a broken tee or dry patch of grass.

I align the club face to that line and I align myself. After one more look at the target, I turn my body and make the swing.

It is an easy way for me to settle into my shot as I play each hole. It also calms me down especially when I am standing on the first tee and playing with people I do not know.

In life, I also have a routine every morning. A repetition. A way to ease my mind into the day. Using the bathroom, brushing my teeth, changing into work clothes, writing on the white board for my wife, watering the plants and making the coffee.

My body appreciates the slow progression and the familiarity.

Repetition in a photograph is good. Repetition in our daily life can prevent a tension headache.

Photography Lesson 11

Be Yourself

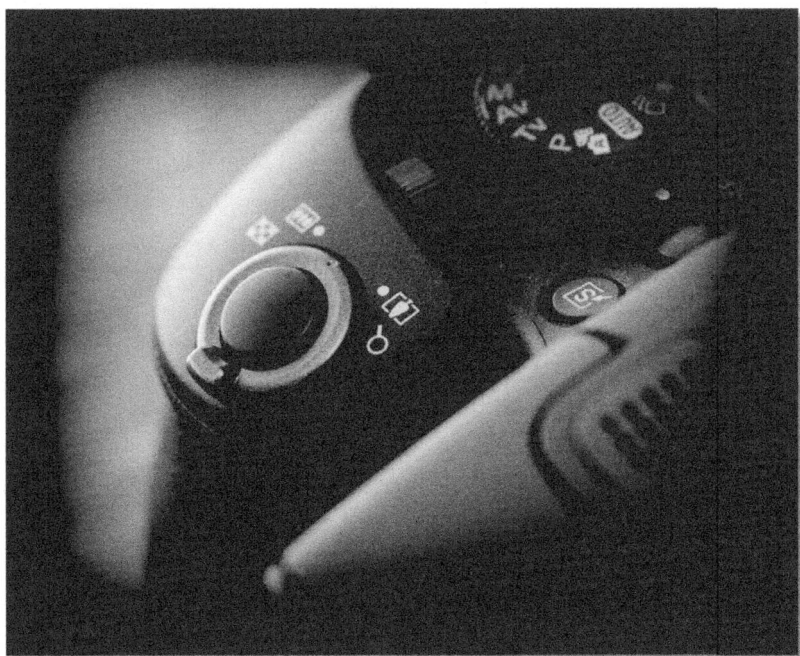

There were many times when I showed my favorite photograph to my wife, she would say, "I don't like it! It is too close."

I love close up shots. She does not.

Looking around in the photography world, there are many styles out there. In my recent trip to Kyoto, I found a photography museum where they were exhibiting photographs with the style I love, close up. I felt like I found some long lost friends. It also solidifies my feeling about being myself and shooting the way I love.

So, be yourself!

"There are always two people in every picture: the photographer and the viewer."
— **Ansel Adams**

Life Strategy 11

I am Who I am

I have been writing poems for many years. I write in English and Chinese.

Last year, I joined a group of poets from southeast Asia. I thought the goal of the group was to share poems. However, I soon found out that some poets wanted to be the teacher or the police officer of the group.

One day, one of them wrote that I do not even know what constitute a poem. It seemed that I needed to write the way they write to call myself a poet and call my writings a poem.

I am who I am. I left the group.

For me, the goal of a photograph or a poem is to communicate. It is all about sharing. I remember the early days of freestyle Chinese poem when after reading a poem, I was left in the dark scratching my head. "What did he say?"

Then there will be articles written by other poets who would explain what the poet meant.

That is too much work. A poem is a poem. It is not a riddle.

Photography Lesson 12

Catch the Feeling

I was going over my photographs from Kyoto last night and found the above picture.

Something stood out when I saw it again. The tree trunk and the thick branch hiding among the pine needles presented a certain kind of feeling.

I posted it in my Facebook page with the following lines:

"Searching
is not a very good word
for someone who is lost
inside himself."

One does not have to be a poet to write lines like that. One has to quiet the mind, settle the heart, open the flow of energy to catch the voice deep from inside.

In that state of mind, you can capture the feeling through your photograph. You can also allow your true self and voice to be expressed.

"Great photography is about depth of feeling, not depth of field."
— **Peter Adams**

Life Strategy 12

Clear Your Mind

The year was 2003. It was late winter. I carried a suitcase and headed for Dallas, Texas. From there, I went to a suburb, checked into a Vipassana Meditation Center where the first thing I did was surrender my cellphone.

After surrendering the cellphone, I committed myself to one hundred hours of clearing my mind. Or should I say, watching my mind. No talking. No interaction with other human beings.

After the thoughts settled, after they gave up and came less frequently, I was able to feel. I was able to really feel the effects of my thoughts and the attached emotions.

Feeling our emotions is important part of being a human being. The trick is, we do not want to be carried away by it.

So many times, we drugged ourselves with alcohol, cigarettes, drugs, loud music, sex and others. We wanted a way to escape. However, what I learned over the years was that we need to deal with our emotions face to face.

Clear the mind and face those emotions, especially the negative ones. The fear, the anger, the hatred, the anxiety and others.

Through meditation, we are centered. We are able to allow the emotions to pass just as we allow the thoughts to pass.

Feel the emotions. Enjoy the good ones. Allow the negative ones to pass.

Photography Lesson 13

Wait for the Perfect Storm

Sometimes we go out with the best intentions of shooting a great photograph. We go out at dawn and dusk where there is perfect light. We go to places where there are known breathtaking sceneries.

However, sometimes we found nothing.

Sometimes we have to be patient like a fisherman holding his fishing pole, waiting for the perfect storm.

When I was in Kyoto recently, I visited the Yasaka Shrine late in the afternoon. The lighting was perfect. The temple with orange and yellow colors became more vibrant with the light from the near setting sun. I found a row of lanterns with lights shining in the right direction. Then I saw two Japanese ladies dressed in kimono having fun taking pictures of each other.

My first thought was to join them. Maybe I could have a picture with them. However, I did not have the courage. After I passed them, I could not help but set my camera in sports mode, turned back and got some consecutive shots.

The result was my favorite photograph: Two playful Japanese ladies in kimono with a row of lanterns.

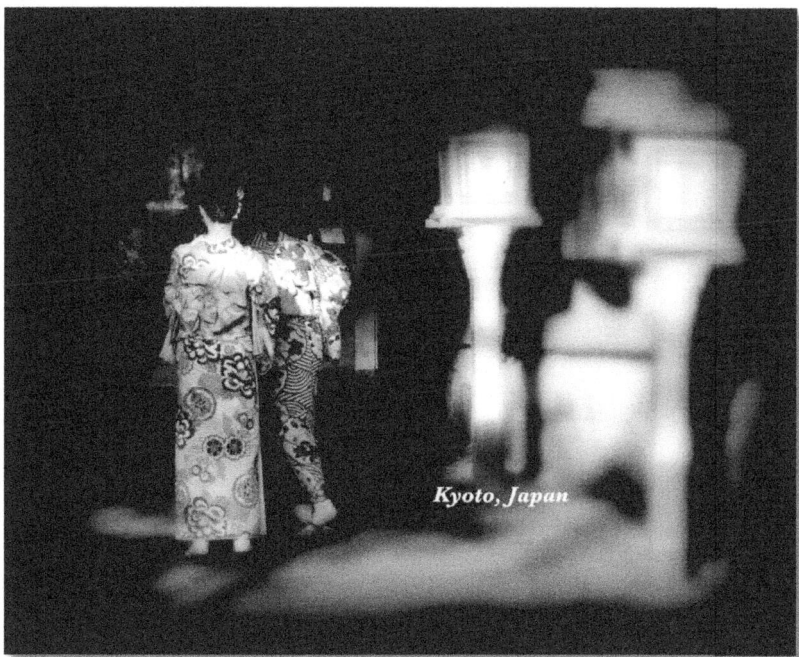

Kyoto, Japan

"Look and think before opening the shutter. The heart and mind are the true lens of the camera."
— **Yousuf Karsh**

Life Strategy 13

Be Patient

We were frequently told to work hard, plan well, execute faithfully and we shall achieve what we want.

That is true.

In life, however, if you live long enough, you noticed that sometimes all your efforts seemed to be futile. Nothing worked. You cannot see the possibility of reaching your goal.

On the other hand, if you are patient enough, if you allow it, serendipity sets in. Everything happens in a blink.

Case in point.

I remember vividly that day in October of 2015. My wife and I were in our rented car, cruising down Las Vegas Boulevard when we started talking about the future again.

At that time, we were living in Albuquerque, New Mexico. We visited Los Angeles and Las Vegas frequently because we miss Chinatown.

She grew up in Taipei, Taiwan and I grew up in Manila, Philippines. One thing we had in common was the need to eat good Chinese food.

I asked the first important question. "What if? What if I give it a try? Maybe there is a job opening here?"

She followed with an event changing answer. "Yes. Why not? Give it a try."

After we went home, I sent a message to my co-intern Dr. Batugal. That was a Monday. He answered back and said that he would contact their recruiter.

The next day, I was off in the afternoon. I got a call from a number I did not recognize. Since I was expecting a call, I answered. It was the recruiter.

The following day, Wednesday, I had a phone interview with one of their medical directors. It was followed by a visit to Las Vegas the following week.

Finally, I got a contract ten days after my initial contact.

Furthermore, we sold our house in eight days. I got my Nevada medical license in thirty days instead of the usual ninety days.

In photography and in life, sometimes, when we least expect, if we are patient enough, a beautiful photograph and a wonderful experience fall into our laps.

And we smile.

Photography Lesson 14

Know Where and When

In the past two years, I renewed my interest in bird watching. For me, it is a three-in-one activity. I get to walk, do my photography and watch birds.

Taking pictures of birds can be tricky. You need to know a little about their habits to find them.

The first question is when. When can I see them? You can see them throughout the day, but early morning and late afternoon will be better. Because that is when they are out hunting for food.

The second question is where. Where can I find them. They love to settle on the tree top. Certain birds like the night heron or the egrets love water.

This morning, I went to the Clark County Wetland Park. I was scanning the tree top when a saw a dark shadow. I knew it must be one of those bigger birds like an eagle or falcon. And I got the following.

Not far from where I found the falcon, I crossed the bridge. I look through the banks of the wash because I know that egrets or night heron might settle there. I did not see anything. Then as I was leaving, something caught my attention. I pointed the camera and found the following.

"Great photography is about depth of feeling, not depth of field."
— **Peter Adams**

Life Strategy 14

Where to find meaning?

I recently learned not to look for happy in life but to look for meaning.

The speaker pointed out four pillars of meaning. Belonging, purpose, transcendence and story telling.

Belonging to a relationship, family and group can help us have meaning in life. I realized that as a writer and photographer, my readers in Facebook formed a community through the internet. I am also very lucky to be happily married to my wife.

As a writer, my purpose is simple. I want to share what I picked up from my surroundings and share it with my readers. As a father, I want to share my knowledge with my children and hope that they can venture into their future with a little ease. As a photographer, I want to share the images I saw in the wild.

And when I do the sharing, I transcend the busyness of the human life. I transcend the turmoil of emotions. Life seems to be a better place to be.

Lastly, as I tell this stories to you, I find meaning, peace and eventually, happiness.

Afterword

One day.

Sensei: So Benjie, what did you learn from writing this book.

Me: A lot. It is all about story telling.

Sensei: Story telling?

Me: Yes. I have been telling the wrong story about myself. I have been saying, "Poor me. Look at poor Benjie. He did all the hard work, climbed the mountain and found out that there was nothing on the mountain top!"

Sensei: And?

Me: And now, the following is the new version.

"Lucky Me"

I was born in Manila, Philippines. It was a place with mixed cultures, where my Chinese ancestry integrated with the local Filipino flavors, plus the influential American dreams.

It was a place where I learned to speak different languages to precipitate different cultures into a well of creativity. I speak Mandarin, Fujian, Tagalog, English and a little Spanish.

My father worked hard. I did not remember a day where we did not have food on the table or a roof over our heads. My mother stayed home to make sure that her seven children were taken cared of.

After my first grade, I went to Taiwan and Hong Kong, my first taste of foreign land. And after my junior year in high school, I went back for another two weeks of visit.

I was blessed to go to a bilingual school where I read books after books in the library. I

completed a whole series about Sherlock Holmes in Chinese. I started writing early, and continued until these days.

The mixed culture of Manila allowed me to became adaptive and very flexible in my adult life. The training grounds of a Boy Scout troop allowed me to bloom from an introvert to an extrovert. The life changing classes in medical school plus the real life experience of residency added my preparation for a career where I make a difference in a patient's life, either saving it or minimizing the pain and suffering.

I belong to a group of professionals whose kind heart is ready to extend a helping hand. The purpose of my life is clear and simple. I educate and help one patient at a time, one day at a time.

And all my travels to live or visit different places expanded my view of this human world. I fell many times but I also stood up again and again. It was all those bruises and scars which made me a good photographer, a good writer and good poet.

I now understand that I am standing on the mountain top seeing the world in a different perspective. The journey was hard but essential. The goal is not to be rich and satisfied at the mountain top. The goal is to reach the top after many years of trial and error. It is the view at the mountain top that is important. It is the enlightenment. It is the AHA moment.

This is the story I want to tell myself again and again from now on. This is the story I want to tell my grandchildren and great grandchildren. This is the story that will give me the meaning of this life.

Again

I rose from my death bed
Carried my old camera
And went back to the room where I was born
Determined to take different pictures

There were scenes which I missed
The light source was bad
I was looking from a wrong angle
I was too impatient

The baby did smile
He was happy to get a chance to breath
To kick his feet
And start an adventure with all emotions

That will bring tears from either
Crying or laughing
That will bring pain from either
Too much or too little to do

And most of all
Taking the right picture
No matter how bad it is
Will tell the right story

Made in the USA
Las Vegas, NV
31 May 2025

22956170R00154